READING STREET

Doing the Right Thing

Program Authors

Connie Juel, Ph.D.

Jeanne R. Paratore, Ed.D.

Deborah Simmons, Ph.D.

Sharon Vaughn, Ph.D.

Glenview, Illinois
Boston, Massachusetts
Chandler, Arizona
Hoboken, New Jersey

ISBN-13: 978-0-328-45293-4
ISBN-10:   0-328-45293-9

10 11 12 13 14 V011 18 17 16 15 14
CC1

Doing the Right Thing

Good Deeds 5

Why is kindness important?

Risk-Takers 31

Why do we help others even if there are risks?

TO THE RESCUE 57

What are the rewards in helping others?

Unselfish Gifts 83

Why do people make sacrifices for others?

We the People... 109

How can people protect freedom?

Good Deeds

Contents

Good Deeds

Words 2 the Wise

Kindness is doing something nice without expecting anything in return. One way to show kindness is by doing good deeds. As you read, think of ways to show kindness.

Kindness

What is kindness? Kindness is showing that we care about another person. A small act or a few words that help another person are kind deeds. The people we help might not even know we have made their lives better. They might not be able to say thanks. We don't do a kind act expecting to get something back. We do it to help others.

When a person might be hurt, find a way to help.

One problem might only take a minute to solve with everyone's help.

The chance to do a kind act turns up every day. The first step is to think about what someone else might need. The next step is to try to help!

Did a friend spill a drink at lunch? Grab some napkins and help clean it up. Did someone trip on a stair? Don't ignore her. Stop and ask, "Are you okay?" Did a classmate lose a favorite hat? Offer to help him look for it.

Kindness could be as easy as helping a new classmate feel welcome.

Look around. There are more ways to be kind. Saying hello to new students in class is a kind act. Did you find a lost jacket or backpack? Turn it in to your school office. Did a teammate make a mistake and drop the ball that you passed to her? Give her a smile and toss her the ball again. It's kind to give people a second chance.

There are many chances to be kind every day right where you are. Others gain a lot when we are considerate. Each small act of kindness is important. Kindness makes life easier. And it makes everyone happier!

These people are doing a good deed by keeping the beach clean for others.

11

Volunteers MAKE A DIFFERENCE

by Dave Brook

Hair, bracelets, and wishes! All of these support others during difficult times. This support is possible because of volunteers. They give time or money to a charity to help others. Volunteers find many ways to make a difference in people's lives!

Locks of Love

Imagine that you are sitting in a barber's chair or a beauty shop. You are getting your hair cut. Will you let those locks of hair be swept away? Some people use their hair to help others.

Volunteers donate at least ten inches of hair to Locks of Love.

Some children have lost their hair because of a sickness. Locks of Love is a charity that helps people support these children. People donate their hair to make wigs for children.

In order to donate, people need to have at least ten inches of their hair cut off. Locks of Love can use hair from men, women, and children. Donors put their bundled hair in a plastic bag. Then they mail it to Locks of Love.

This girl lost her hair because of a sickness.

Now she has lots of hair thanks to Locks of Love.

Experts can turn this long hair into a wig for a child.

orial Heath Systems
ocor fr Love Day
an 7, 2005

The organization passes the donated hair to experts who turn the hair into beautiful wigs. Then they give these hairpieces to children who can't afford them.

Adults and children all over the world are donating their hair to Locks of Love. Children who wear the hairpieces feel happy and confident. The people who donate are happy that they could help.

It's All in the Wrist

Earrings, necklaces, rings, and bracelets are accessories. Stretchy wristbands are colorful. They are fashionable and popular. Most people wear them to look better. Some people wear them to make a statement. But what are they really all about?

The Lance Armstrong Foundation was the first charity to make stretchy wristbands popular. Lance Armstrong is an athlete who survived cancer. He started a campaign to help cancer survivors.

These bracelets can be stylish. But they also make a statement.

When you donate one dollar to the campaign, you receive a yellow bracelet. *LiveStrong* is written on it. The money supports research and education about cancer.

The Lance Armstrong Foundation is the main organization that supports the campaign. Its volunteers often have cancer. And many are cancer survivors. The bracelets remind them of what the foundation believes. It says that "Unity is strength, knowledge is power, and attitude is everything."

The Lance Armstrong Foundation encourages cancer survivors to share their experiences with others.

The Make-A-Wish Foundation grants many children's wishes.

Make a Wish

The Make-A-Wish Foundation was started in 1980. Its volunteers grant wishes to children who are seriously ill. They try to be considerate of these children. They find out a child's special wish. Then the volunteers make the wish come true!

The foundation chooses children between the ages of two-and-a-half and eighteen. They have a sickness that threatens their lives. Family, friends, and doctors can nominate* a child. Volunteers raise about $7,000 for each wish.

*nominate to suggest someone

What do most children wish for?

Children usually have four types of wishes.

1. *I wish to meet . . .*

Many children want to meet their favorite movie star, athlete, or musician.

2. *I wish to be . . .*

Children get the opportunity to be someone for a day. Two popular choices are firefighter and police officer.

3. *I wish to have . . .*

Children often wish for a dream gift, such as a tree house.

4. *I wish to go . . .*

Children often want to attend an important event or explore an exciting place.

The Make-A-Wish Foundation gives children an experience to remember.

Celeste Dominique was Princess-for-a-Day thanks to the Make-A-Wish Foundation.

The foundation is committed to making wishes come true.

This girl is living her dream of caring for horses.

More than 25,000 volunteers worldwide give their time to the Make-A-Wish Foundation. These volunteers help raise money to fulfill the dreams of many children.

Volunteers think of creative ways to be considerate of others. They find many ways to show they care. Then they take action to help!

WHAT DO YOU THINK?

How are Locks of Love, the Lance Armstrong Foundation, and the Make-A-Wish Foundation similar? How are they different?

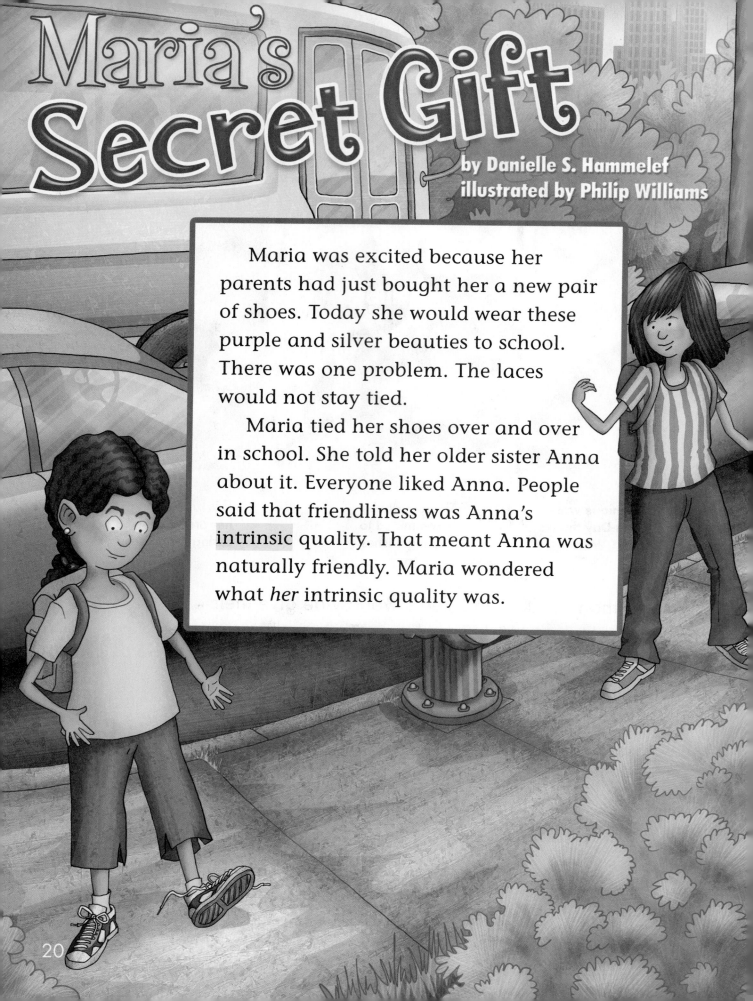

Maria's Secret Gift

by Danielle S. Hammelef
illustrated by Philip Williams

Maria was excited because her parents had just bought her a new pair of shoes. Today she would wear these purple and silver beauties to school. There was one problem. The laces would not stay tied.

Maria tied her shoes over and over in school. She told her older sister Anna about it. Everyone liked Anna. People said that friendliness was Anna's intrinsic quality. That meant Anna was naturally friendly. Maria wondered what *her* intrinsic quality was.

On the way home Maria saw a lady at the corner. She was staring across the street.

That lady needs help, thought Maria, as she tied her shoelaces. *But how can I help?*

As Maria rose, she saw that the *Walk* signal had lit up. The lady was crossing the street toward her. "Thank you. It was fortunate you were there," the lady said when she came near. *Why did the lady thank me?* Maria wondered.

Maria ran to catch up to Anna. She was at the barbershop when she had to stop again. She leaned against the open door to tie her shoe. When it started to slam shut, Maria almost fell.

22

Maria regained her balance and finished tying her shoe. As she stood up, a skateboarder whizzed by.

"Thanks," he said.

Maria's mouth dropped open. *Thank you? Again?*

Maria shook her head and began running. She had nearly reached home when she saw Ms. Sanchez standing next to a car. Usually, she was busy restoring old cars. Now she looked confused. Maria jogged over.

"Hi, Ms. Sanchez. Is something wrong with the car?" asked Maria.

"Yes. A round metal part that I need is missing," replied Ms. Sanchez.

Maria leaned against the car to tie her shoes. Suddenly, she heard Ms. Sanchez shout, "Thanks! You found it!"

"What?" Maria exclaimed. But Ms. Sanchez had ducked under the hood and was busy with repairs.

Maria raced home. Maybe she had special powers! Was this *her* intrinsic quality?

When Maria got home, her mother and sister were standing by the washing machine. The machine wasn't working.

"Mom! I have special powers!" she blurted out.

Mom kept pushing dials, but one eyebrow went up. "What makes you think so?"

"On the way home, three people thanked me for no reason at all!" said Maria.

"What were you doing when they said that?" asked Mom.

"Tying my shoes," said Maria.

Maria continued. "First, there was a lady who crossed the street and said thanks. Next, a skateboarder said thanks when he didn't crash into the barbershop door. Then, Ms. Sanchez thanked me for finding her car part! It always happened when I was tying my shoes. See! They're untied again!"

Maria bent over once more and bumped into the washing machine. It suddenly started! Mom's face lit up!

"How fortunate for those people! Did you bump anything when you bent to tie your shoelaces?" Mom grinned.

"Oh, I must have bumped into the Walk button on the traffic signal and the barbershop door too. I must have made the part drop when I leaned on Ms. Sanchez's car," Maria said.

"So you don't have special powers at all! You've been doing kind deeds by accident!" said Mom. And they all laughed.

What Do You Think?

Why did Maria think good things were happening? What was the real reason?

27

How Did THAT Happen?

ILLUSTRATED BY BILL VANN

Everyone needs help at times. Lots of people want to be the ones who help. But would you want Stevie, Kelly, and Arnie to help you?

4 you 2 Do

Word Play

Choose one of this week's concept vocabulary words and write a short wristband message.

Making Connections

What do Locks of Love, the Lance Armstrong Foundation, the Make-A-Wish Foundation, and Maria have in common? How are they different?

On Paper

Invent a new organization that does kind acts. Create a name that will make people want to be volunteers. Explain how the organization will help others.

Contents

Risk-Takers

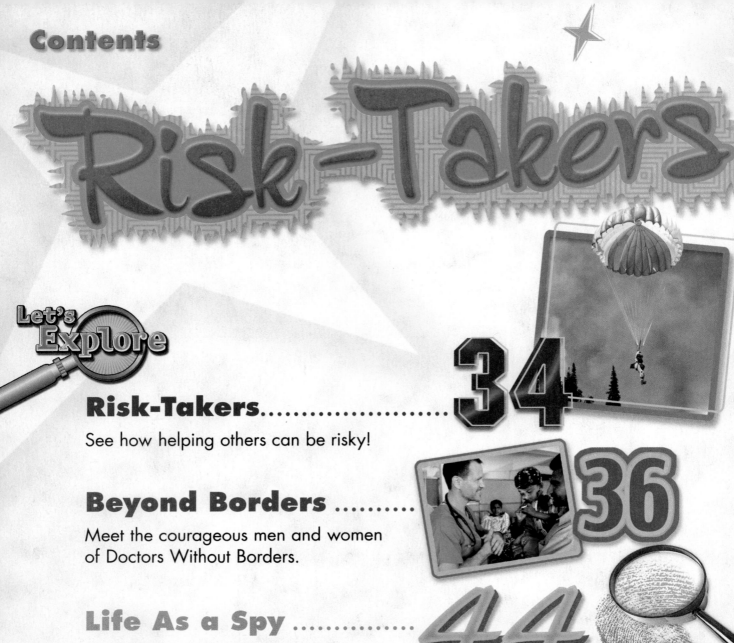

Let's Explore

Words 2 the Wise

Risk-takers put themselves in danger to help others. As you read, think about what it means to take risks to help others.

Let's Explore

RISK

The Coast Guard often goes on dangerous water rescue missions.

Smokejumpers are a special kind of firefighter. They battle wild fires.

Some doctors take risks to bring medical care to people in far-off places.

34

TAKERS

A firefighter rushes into a burning building to rescue a trapped child. A doctor rides a helicopter into a distant village to help people who are sick.

Many people have risky jobs that help others. Some volunteer their time. They work to keep others healthy and safe. They work to prevent crimes. The risks they take help make our lives safer.

Why do people take risks to help others? Many do it because they want to make a difference. Sometimes, people do not realize the danger. They just think about helping.

People who put their own lives in danger to help others are often called brave and courageous. They take risks because they want to do what's right.

Beyond Borders

MEDECINS
SANS FRONTIERES

by Michelle Schaub

Médecins Sans Frontières is French for Doctors Without Borders.

In 1971 a group of doctors in France started a group called Doctors Without Borders. They wanted to help people in the world who needed doctors but couldn't get to them. Many of these people lived in places that were torn apart by war. The French doctors didn't care about countries or borders. They wanted to help people on both sides of a war.

Refugees in Ethiopia and a member of Doctors Without Borders

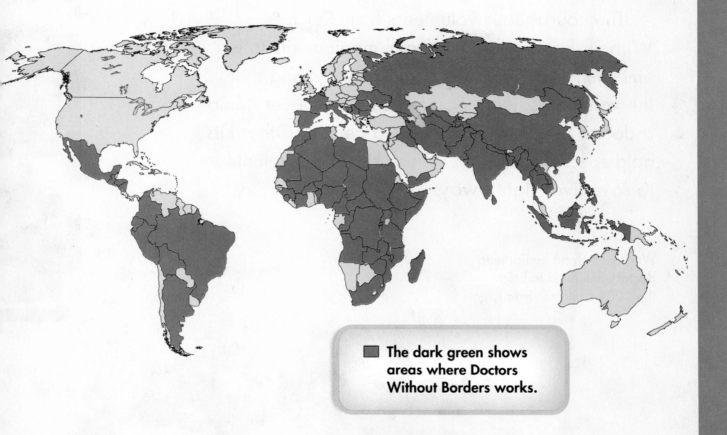

The dark green shows areas where Doctors Without Borders works.

Today, Doctors Without Borders has over 3,000 volunteers. These volunteers work in 80 countries. They often work in dangerous places. They don't have time to worry about the risks. They are too busy saving lives.

IN CASE OF EMERGENCY

When disaster strikes, volunteers from Doctors Without Borders are often the first to arrive. Sometimes an emergency happens because of a war. Sometimes an emergency is the result of a natural disaster. There is always risk. But Doctors Without Borders rushes to intervene.

The courageous volunteers from Doctors Without Borders bring special medical kits to emergencies. These kits contain everything that the volunteers need. Some kits contain everything a doctor needs to operate on a person. Other kits hold special medicines. These kits allow volunteers to save lives right away.

Workers unload equipment doctors will need to help the 2004 tsunami victims.

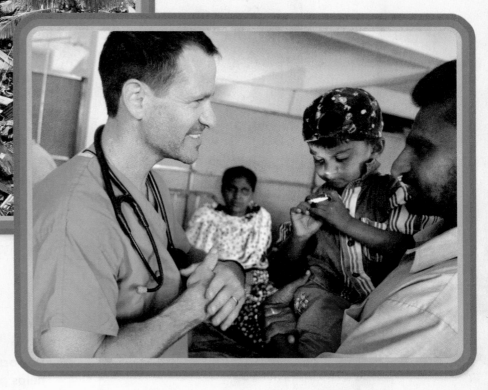

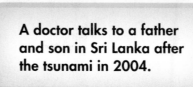

A doctor talks to a father and son in Sri Lanka after the tsunami in 2004.

In December 2004, a deadly tsunami* (soo-NAH-mee) struck the coasts of many Asian countries. Doctors Without Borders rushed to help. Dr. Claire Rieux (REE-uh) is a volunteer with the group. She made an excursion to a hospital in Indonesia. Many of the doctors who worked at the hospital were lost in the tsunami. Dr. Rieux and her team worked day and night to treat victims of the tsunami. They helped save many lives.

*tsunami a very large and destructive ocean wave caused by an underwater earthquake

Doctors Without Borders helps people who have left their homes because of wars or hunger.

Doctors Without Borders does not only intervene during emergencies. It also helps in countries where people can't get to doctors or hospitals. The group provides many beneficial services to the people who live in these places. Volunteers start medical clinics. They train local staff. They hand out medicine.

HELPING IN OTHER WAYS

The main goal of Doctors Without Borders is to give medical care. But the group also provides many other beneficial services.

Dr. Sylvaine Blanty (SILL-vayn BLAHN-tee) volunteers at a Doctors Without Borders clinic in Niger (NY-jer), Africa. Thousands of children in Niger are very sick because of hunger. The clinic Dr. Blanty works in is a special feeding center.

A volunteer with Doctors Without Borders treats children in Niger.

Dr. Blanty helps children get healthy. Many children are too weak to talk when they first arrive. With the help of Dr. Blanty and her staff, these children will get better soon.

Liz Walker is a water specialist for Doctors Without Borders. She has made excursions to places like Tibet. She helps places solve problems with their water. Many people in Tibet are drinking dirty water. The water is full of deadly germs. It makes them very sick.

An aid worker from Doctors Without Borders works in Afghanistan.

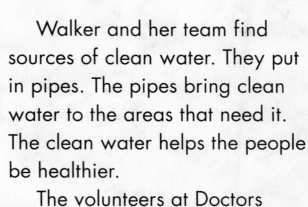

Walker and her team find sources of clean water. They put in pipes. The pipes bring clean water to the areas that need it. The clean water helps the people be healthier.

The volunteers at Doctors Without Borders travel all over the world to help people who are hurt or sick. They might bring medical care. They might bring food. They might bring clean water. Whatever they do, these volunteers are courageous. And borders do not limit them.

Volunteers for Doctors Without Borders make a difference in many lives.

What Do You Think?

What kinds of risks do volunteers for Doctors Without Borders take?

Life as a Spy

as a SPY

BY MIKE BRESNAHAN

The movies make the life of a spy seem full of adventures. But sometimes a spy is just an ordinary person. Three ordinary people worked as spies to serve their countries in unusual ways.

Seeing Double

James Armistead Lafayette (lah-fee-ET) was an African American slave. He lived during the Revolutionary War. James wanted America to be free from Great Britain. He asked his master for permission to help the American cause. James became a spy for the American army.

James was sent behind enemy lines. His job was to spy on a British leader named General Cornwallis (korn-WAWL-is). James worked in Cornwallis's camp. He pretended to be an escaped slave. James overheard many secrets.

Cornwallis asked James to spy on the Americans. Now James was a double spy! He pretended to work for the British, but James stayed loyal to the Americans. James fooled Cornwallis by telling him false secrets.

James Armistead Lafayette worked as an American spy during the Revolutionary War.

British and American spies wrote letters in secret codes to disguise what they were saying.

Lafayette's work helped bring about Cornwallis's surrender at Yorktown, shown here.

James's work as a double spy was risky, but it helped the Americans win the Battle of Yorktown. James risked his life for America's freedom. In return, James Armistead Lafayette was later granted his own freedom.

"The Beardless Boy"

Frank Thompson was a spy during the Civil War. Thompson stole secrets from the Confederate army. But Thompson also had a secret. He was really a woman named Sarah Emma Edmonds.

When the Civil War started, Sarah, known as Emma, became a nurse. But she felt that she could help more if she were actually in the army.

So Emma cut her hair short. She dressed as a man and joined the Union army as Frank Thompson.

Sarah Emma Edmonds joined the war to care for sick and wounded soldiers.

Sarah Emma Edmonds as Frank Thompson.

Emma, disguised as Frank, started as a nurse in camp hospitals. This job brought her behind enemy lines. She kept her eyes and ears open. She gave information to the Union generals. The generals decided that Emma, whom they knew as Frank, would make a good spy.

As a spy, Emma went on many secret missions. Each time, she would pose as another person. Emma became a master of disguise.

Once, Emma posed as a peddler.* Each time Emma went undercover she discovered facts about the Confederates' plans. This information was very beneficial to the Union army.

Emma took many risks to get Confederate secrets. But she kept her biggest secret to herself. The Union army did not discover the true identity of Frank Thompson until after the Civil War was over. Sarah Emma Edmonds was buried with full military honors for her bravery.

*peddler someone who travels from place to place selling things

Emma could disguise herself as Frank and transform back to herself in a flash.

Good Wood

Fritz Kolbe was a quiet German citizen. He lived during World War II. Kolbe disagreed with Adolf Hitler's ideas. Kolbe worked for the government. At work he learned many of Hitler's secrets.

He knew he could use these secrets to help Germany become free from Hitler's rule. Kolbe decided to share these secrets. He contacted an American agent. The agent decided Kolbe would make a good spy. He gave Kolbe the code name George Wood.

CONFI

Year: 1943

Name: Fritz Kolbe

Alias: George Wood

Job: Spy

Cover: Quiet, German citizen

Fritz Kolbe, also known as George Wood, was a German who spied for the Americans during World War II.

In Germany, George Wood made copies of information about Hitler. Then he sent the information to the Americans. If George Wood had been discovered, he would have been killed. By the end of the war, George Wood had passed 2,600 documents to the Americans.

James Armistead Lafayette, Sarah Emma Edmonds, and Fritz Kolbe were all successful spies. They took many risks to help others.

NTIAL

What Do You Think?

How can a spy's work be risky?

Ask Addy

Write to Addy Vizer, a junior at East High School. Addy offers advice on how to make tough decisions.

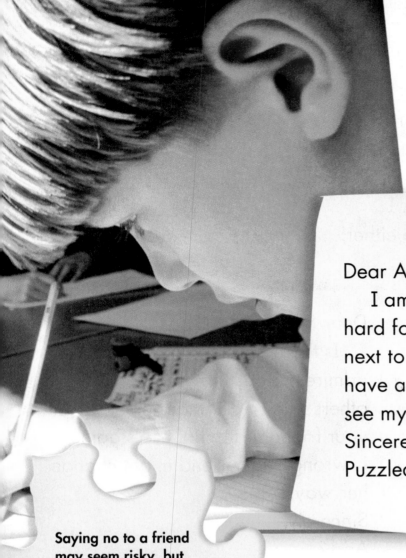

Dear Addy,

    I am pretty good at math. It is hard for my friend, James. He sits next to me in class. Whenever we have a math test, James wants to see my paper. What should I do?

Sincerely,

Puzzled over Math

Saying no to a friend may seem risky, but cheating is wrong.

Dear Puzzled over Math,

    Before the next test, help James study. You can help James so he won't need to copy from you. On test day, your only job is to take your own test.

Sincerely,

Addy

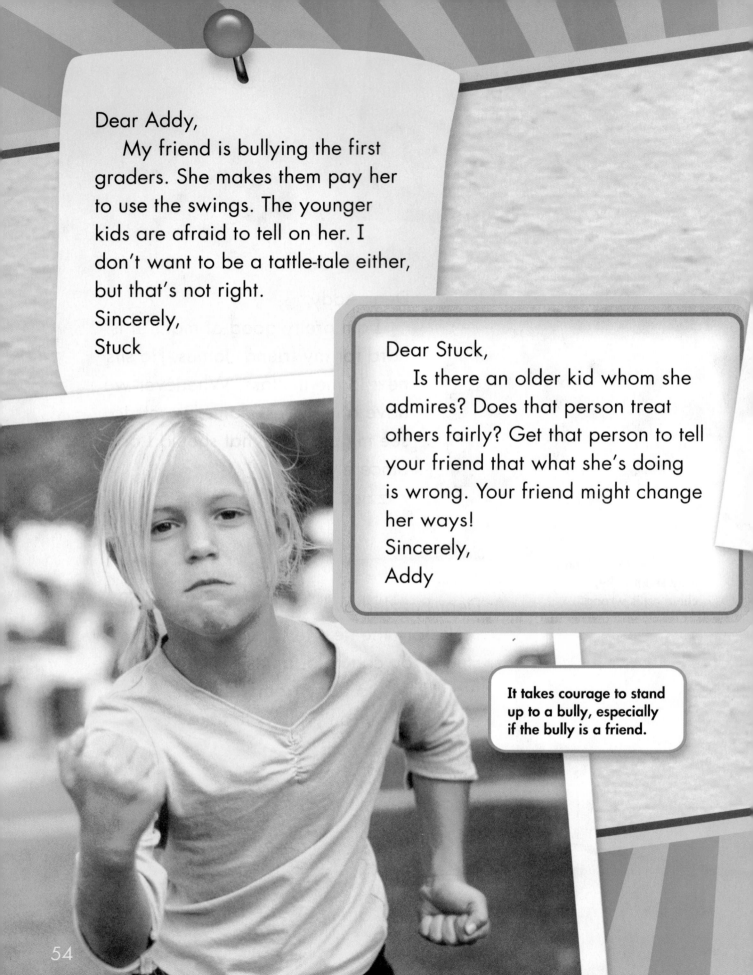

Dear Addy,
My friend is bullying the first graders. She makes them pay her to use the swings. The younger kids are afraid to tell on her. I don't want to be a tattle-tale either, but that's not right.
Sincerely,
Stuck

Dear Stuck,
Is there an older kid whom she admires? Does that person treat others fairly? Get that person to tell your friend that what she's doing is wrong. Your friend might change her ways!
Sincerely,
Addy

It takes courage to stand up to a bully, especially if the bully is a friend.

Making everyone feel welcome can be a challenge.

Dear Addy,
    I have a tree fort. My best friend and I chill there. I invited a new guy from our block to the fort. My best friend got mad and says he won't be my friend. How can I be friends with them both?
Sincerely,
Tree for Three

Dear Tree for Three,
    Ask your best friend to agree to invite the new boy to the tree house one time. Tell him that you will agree to do something that he wants. Tell him that you will always be his friend.
Sincerely,
Addy

55

4 you 2 Do

Word Play

Complete each sentence below
with a concept vocabulary word.

1. Information about the enemy
   can be _____ to the other side.
2. Taking a risk to help others
   is _____.
3. Spies must _____ as other
   people to get information.

Making Connections

The volunteers for Doctors Without
Borders take risks. Undercover spies
take risks. What are the risks and
rewards of both types of work?

On Paper

People such as Doctors Without
Borders and spies risk their lives
to help others. But you don't have
to risk your life to be courageous.
What are some everyday ways
to be courageous?

TO THE RESCUE

Contents

TO THE RESCUE

+ American Red Cross

Words 2 the Wise

There are many different ways to come to the rescue and help others. As you read, think about simple ways of **helping others** every day.

Helpful

Horseback riding is fun. Riding horses also can help children with disabilities. The children practice balance and must think clearly to make the horses obey.

Once, people thought that these kids would never be able to ride, but they can with assistance. Other kids help them!

Volunteers walk next to the horses as the children ride. The volunteers make sure the riders are safe and having fun.

Volunteers walk alongside riders.

Horses

Other tasks are important too. Some volunteers scrub and put away all the equipment. Some are stable workers. They brush and wash the horses.

These kids show up and do their jobs. The riders depend on them. It's a lot of responsibility. Many volunteers work so that a few children can get help with their disabilities.

HELPING HANDS

by Liese Vogel

Meet Joe. Right now he and his family are staring at their house. A hurricane has torn off the roof and knocked down a wall. Joe feels panic. Everything's gone! Where will his family go? They have always lived near the coast of Florida.

Meet Mary. She lives in Michigan. She reads about the hurricane and learns that the damage is terrible! Is relief on the way?

Hurricanes form on the ocean and move onto land.

After a hurricane, police, firefighters, and other community workers rush to help. They are trained to handle emergencies. The first job is to rescue people who are stranded or hurt. Joe and his family are stranded. They wait with their neighbors for assistance.

Red Cross volunteers arrive next. They bring food and supplies to provide relief. The U.S. government is sending equipment for building tents and other shelters.

Police and firefighters face the worst conditions when they arrive at a disaster site.

During a hurricane, forceful winds blow apart buildings.

Heavy rains from hurricanes cause floods.

For Joe and his family, the first hours are the roughest. Fallen trees, sections of buildings, or overturned cars block streets. Some streets are flooded. Joe doesn't want to enter his house because it may be dangerous. Joe looks at other houses and hopes no one is trapped.

Back in Michigan, Mary is watching the trucks on TV and wondering how she can help.

Joe and his family go to the high school gymnasium. It is now a shelter. The relief workers unload food there. Volunteers serve dinners and set up cots. They tell Joe's family that there will be a place for them to sleep.

Back in Michigan, Mary watches the news. She is glad that help has arrived. Mary remembers that she knows first aid, and she was also trained to drive a truck. She wonders how she can become a volunteer.

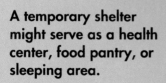
A temporary shelter might serve as a health center, food pantry, or sleeping area.

People who live far from a disaster want to help. Some are worried about their relatives who might be near a flood or hurricane.

The Red Cross trains volunteers to be relief workers. Some workers will need only six hours of training. Others need more than 40 hours. These trained volunteers know how to give assistance fast.

Sometimes families are separated during a disaster. The Red Cross gathers information about disaster victims and puts the information on the Internet. They also send lists of victims to hospitals and shelters so that families can reunite, or find each other.

In Michigan, Mary decides that the next day she will find a way to get involved. Maybe she can donate money. Maybe she can reunite families or make deliveries. Maybe she can travel away from her home and work with the victims.

Mary is sure she would be good at serving meals and giving first aid. No matter what, Mary is determined to help.

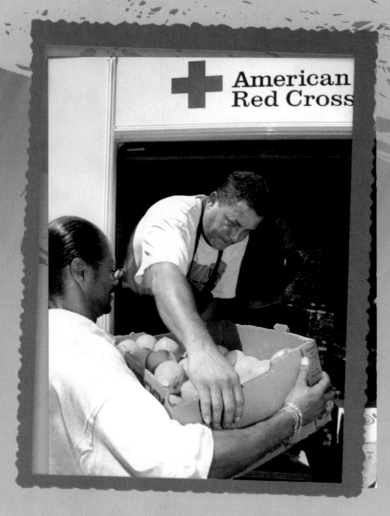

Red Cross workers are trained to drive trucks, build shelters, and distribute food.

The next morning Joe and his family line up for a warm breakfast. Yesterday was the scariest day of their lives. It was full of panic.

Soon, Joe and his wife will find out that aid groups are bringing trailer homes for hurricane victims. Volunteers are arranging for children to return to nearby schools. Joe knows that they must begin to rebuild their lives.

Habitat for Humanity is a group that builds homes for disaster victims. The builders are volunteers.

At the same time, Mary has decided to donate money. Later that day, she will sign up to drive a delivery truck so that supplies can reach people like Joe. Mary and Joe will never meet. But Joe may get some supplies that Mary helped buy or deliver. Groups like the Red Cross make starting over a little easier.

These kids are far away from a disaster, but they are raising money to help.

WHAT DO YOU THINK?

How is the help that Mary can give like the help of the relief groups? How is it different?

Pass, Shoot, SCORE!

by Michael Archer • illustrated by Meredith Johnson

There was only a minute left to play. Sandra jumped up and down.

"Me!" she called. "Throw the ball to me, Deb!"

Debbie frowned and threw the ball to Courtney. Sandra groaned in distress. Courtney was the clumsiest player on the team. She missed, and the whistle blew. The Cougars had lost to the Raccoons, 78 to 54.

"Hey, why didn't you throw the ball to me?" Sandra said as they headed into the locker room.

"Because," Debbie said, "you're the biggest ball hog I've ever met!"

"Winning is the most important thing, and you passed to Courtney, the worst player on the team!" said Sandra.

Courtney heard Sandra. She grabbed her backpack and ran out of the locker room.

"Nice going," said Alicia. "We'd all be happier if we played more like a team."

Just then, Coach Mendoza called Sandra into
her office near the locker room.

"Sandra, I need to talk to you," she said. "Mr.
Jones tells me you're failing science. He said you
haven't completed an important assignment."
Coach looked more distressed than Sandra. "Listen
carefully. If this continues, you won't be able to
play basketball on this team anymore."

"But the team can't win without me!"
Sandra exclaimed.

Before the bell the next day, Sandra met with her
science teacher.

"Mr. Jones," she said, "Coach says I need to get
my grades up in your class, or I'm off the team."

"Turn in your science project," Mr. Jones said.
"On time," he added, looking right at Sandra.

"I know. I'll do better. I promise." Sandra wished
that writing were as easy as shooting free throws.
"Thank you for your time," she said as she left.

Sandra left the classroom. She wasn't watching where she was going and crashed into Debbie and Alicia.

"Hey, watch it!" they said.

"Oh! I'm sorry. If I don't improve my science grade, I can't play basketball," Sandra said.

Suddenly, Sandra thought of something. "Debbie, you love science! Will you help me with my project? I don't know how to start."

"You'll need a topic first. But I just can't think of any good ideas right now," Debbie said.

"But you should ask Courtney. She has a lot of great ideas. Hey, Courtney!" she said as Courtney came out of the music room. "Sandra wants to ask you something."

"Me?" said Courtney suspiciously.

Sandra took a breath. "If I don't finish my science project, I'm off the team," she said. "Will you help me? I really need your assistance."

"That's the silliest thing I've ever heard!" said Courtney. "Me? Help you?"

"I'm sorry I was rude, but if you please help me, I'll help you with shooting."

"Well, I guess it's worth a try," said Courtney.

"I really appreciate it!" said Sandra.

Courtney did help. Soon science began to make sense to Sandra. With Courtney's help she got a B on her next test. Sandra was proud of her science project. She earned an A on it.

"I didn't know you'd catch on so quickly," Courtney told her with a grin.

Sandra was happy that Courtney had improved on the basketball court too.

At the next game, the other girls were surprised when Courtney made two baskets. They were even more surprised when Sandra passed the ball instead of hogging it. When the final whistle blew, the score was Cougars 70, Eagles 69.

"We won!" yelled Debbie, giving Courtney a big hug. "You were fantastic!"

"We were all fantastic," said Courtney.

"That's right," said Sandra. "We make a great team!"

WHAT DO YOU THINK?

How was the help Sandra and Courtney gave each other the same? How was it different?

When you see these symbols, one thing's for sure.
Help is on the way! Courageous workers save the day!

 **FEMA**

 American Red Cross

The President oversees the Federal Emergency Management Agency (FEMA). FEMA helps people find places to live after a disaster. It gives people money to replace what they've lost. It helps them return to work. FEMA helps rebuild cities.

The American Red Cross is another group that helps during emergencies. This group hands out food, water, and other supplies. It sets up shelters and helps people find each other.

THE WAY!

HUMANITARIAN LIFELINE TO THE WORLD

National Organization for Victim Assistance

AmeriCares® provides help to people who need emergency medical care. They ship medicine and medical supplies all over the world. This aid goes to people in disaster areas and in war zones.

The police help victims at the scene of a crime. But many victims continue to be scared after a crisis. They can turn to the National Organization for Victim Assistance (NOVA). The organization has a hotline number. Victims can call and talk to counselors to help them recover.

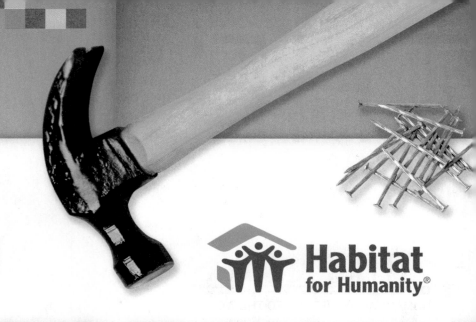

America's
Second Harvest® The Nation's
Food Bank Network™

Ending Hunger.

Habitat
for Humanity®

America's Second Harvest® gives food all year long. It encourages people to volunteer at food banks and donate vegetables and fruits from their own gardens. It also asks larger groups for donations. It works with farmers, food companies, restaurants, and the government.

Habitat for Humanity® builds housing with people who cannot afford to buy a house. One of its strongest supporters is former President Jimmy Carter. Habitat volunteers work together to build homes for families in need. The homeowners pay for the homes that they help to build with the volunteers.

Red kettles and ringing bells tell people The Salvation Army® is near. Bell ringers invite people to throw change into the kettle. This money helps The Salvation Army provide disaster relief. It also collects clothing and other items. The Salvation Army sends these goods to disaster areas.

The United Way sets aside money for disaster aid. This money pays for school supplies, food, building materials, housing, busing, or healthcare for those affected by disasters.

4 YOU 2 DO

Word Play

Read each sentence below. Then choose the concept word or words that are related.

- Help me!
- We have no way to get home from this deserted island!
- Aaaah! What should I do? Whom should I call? Where should I go?

Making Connections

Helping can be just as rewarding as giving. How is this true for the people you read about in "Helping Hands" and "Pass, Shoot, Score!"?

On Paper

Write about a time that you chose to help someone and how you helped. Tell what happened.

Possible answers for Word Play: assistance, stranded, panic

Unselfish Gifts

Contents

Unselfish Gifts

Choose an activity to explore this week's concept—Unselfish Gifts!

Words 2 the Wise

Many people **make sacrifices** to help others. They give their time and talents. They do whatever they can. As you read, think about the ways people give of themselves.

Let's Explore Unselfish

Sharing a lunch can be an unselfish gift.

Suppose a classmate forgets to bring a lunch and you are aware that he has no money with him to buy one. You have a lunch. Will you share it? If you sacrifice, or give up, half of your lunch, you may end up feeling a little hungry. But you'll feel good knowing you helped someone out.

Gifts

When we make a sacrifice, we give up something of value to help someone else. We put someone else's needs ahead of our own.

Some people sacrifice time, effort, or money. They do these things because they feel compassion for others who need help. Each unselfish act is like a gift. What unselfish gifts might you give to others?

This girl sacrifices some free time to help out at the library.

Reaching Out

by Ahmed Habash

People reach out to others in many different ways. They show compassion by donating time, talents, pets, and more!

Therapy* Dogs

Staying in the hospital isn't much fun. You're sick. Family members can't always be near. But wait! Something just walked in the door. It has a furry face and a wagging tail. It's a therapy dog!

**therapy* treatment that helps a person feel better or heal after an illness or accident

A visit from a therapy dog brings a smile.

A good therapy dog is calm.

Most dog owners are aware that petting a dog is comforting. That's why some train their dogs to be therapy dogs. Together they visit people in hospitals, nursing homes, and schools. They sacrifice their time to brighten someone else's day. As one therapy dog owner said, "There is a magic that happens between people and animals." The dogs often draw smiles and giggles from those they visit.

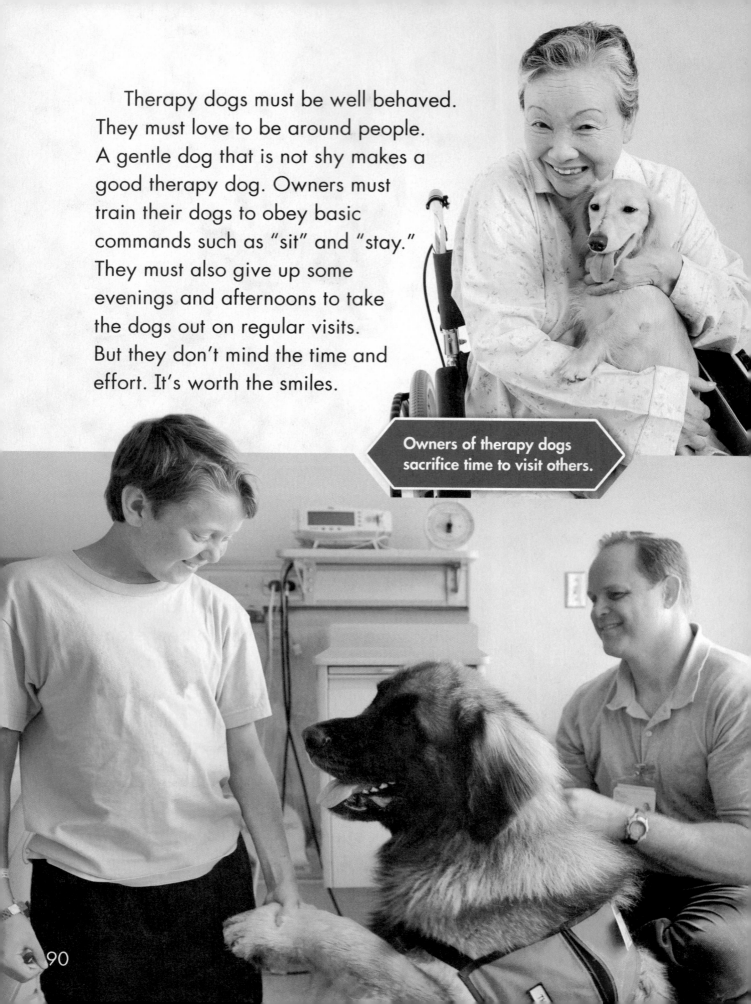

Therapy dogs must be well behaved. They must love to be around people. A gentle dog that is not shy makes a good therapy dog. Owners must train their dogs to obey basic commands such as "sit" and "stay." They must also give up some evenings and afternoons to take the dogs out on regular visits. But they don't mind the time and effort. It's worth the smiles.

Owners of therapy dogs sacrifice time to visit others.

The National Guard helps people when floods, hurricanes, and other disasters strike.

The National Guard

It's the weekend. It's time to relax and have fun with friends and family, right? Not if you're in the National Guard! Members of the Guard give up one weekend every month to train for a special role in helping our country. They sacrifice their free time to be ready to help people in distress.

Members of the National Guard must be strong.

The National Guard is a branch of the United States military. Sometimes Guard members must serve as soldiers, but usually their job is to protect lives and property in times of disaster.

Guard members receive lots of training. They need to be able to meet many kinds of challenges. Some members also have special skills. They might be doctors, engineers, or pilots. They use these skills when they are sent on missions.

Guard members help people in other countries too.

Guard members swing into action quickly. In 2008, thousands of National Guard members were sent to parts of Texas and Louisiana after Hurricane Ike blew through these states. The members provided food, water, and shelter for people affected by the storm. They also helped clean up damaged areas.

Members of the Guard have to sacrifice. But they know they are helping keep people safe and secure. That gives them a feeling of value and pride.

Organ Donors

   Could a single unselfish gift change a person's life forever? Every year, thousands of people make a decision that saves a life. They donate one of their kidneys to another person. People are born with two kidneys, but a person can be healthy with just one.

   The kidneys are important organs because they filter wastes from the blood. Some diseases cause a person's kidneys to fail. To get well, the person needs a new kidney.

People who receive a new kidney can lead very active lives.

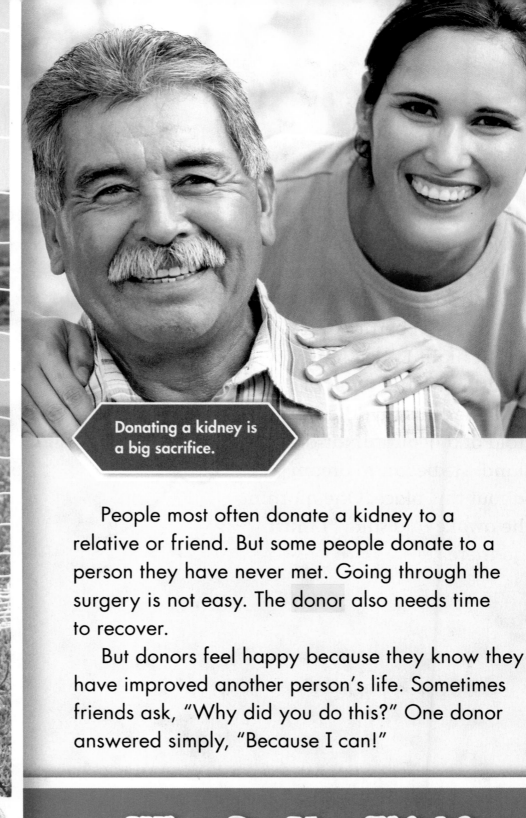

Donating a kidney is a big sacrifice.

People most often donate a kidney to a relative or friend. But some people donate to a person they have never met. Going through the surgery is not easy. The donor also needs time to recover.

But donors feel happy because they know they have improved another person's life. Sometimes friends ask, "Why did you do this?" One donor answered simply, "Because I can!"

What Do You Think?

What sacrifices did you read about?
What makes them sacrifices?

THE STORY OF JUMPING

a Native American folk tale retold by Rufus Dean • illustrated by Mike Reed

Little Mouse had never been far from home. He lived in a grassy spot near the prairie. He was a busy mouse, always searching and sniffing. With his brothers, he gathered berries and seeds.

At night Little Mouse loved to listen to the stories of the old ones. His favorite story told of a beautiful far-off land. He began to dream about this place. One morning he awoke and said, "I must go there."

MOUSE

Little Mouse's brothers were alarmed. "Are you aware of the danger in the prairie?" they asked. "How will you ever find the far-off land?" But Little Mouse knew that he had to go. His brothers could not keep him from his mission.

Early the next morning, Little Mouse set off. He walked and walked. He used his keen eyes to find his way. At day's end, he came to a big river. "How will I ever get across?" he sighed.

"Who are you?" a croaky voice suddenly asked.

Little Mouse spied a large, green frog in the water.

"My name is Little Mouse," he replied. "I'm trying
to get to the far-off land."

"You have a hard journey ahead of you," said Frog.
"You will need a special power—and a new name."

Little Mouse wondered what the frog meant.

"Jump as high as you can," Frog commanded.

Little Mouse did as he was told. He was surprised at how high he jumped. Looking down, he discovered that he now had long, powerful hind legs.

"I name you Jumping Mouse," Frog said.

"How can I ever thank you?" said the humble mouse.

"Here," said Frog. "Hop onto this leaf. I will push you across the river."

When they reached the other side, Frog wished him well. He said, "Do not give up hope, no matter what happens."

Jumping Mouse traveled day and night. Thanks to his new, long legs, he traveled fast. In the daytime, he kept an eye on the sky. He did not want to be eaten by an eagle. Whenever he spotted one, his heart raced. But even though he was afraid, he wondered what it would be like to soar like an eagle.

One day Jumping Mouse stopped to rest by a clump of grass. He soon heard an awful groaning. He slowly crept toward the sound. It was a huge buffalo lying in the grass.

"What is the matter?" Jumping Mouse asked.

"I am blind and cannot find water," the buffalo said.

Jumping Mouse felt compassion for the great beast. He told the buffalo about his journey. He also told him about the power Frog had given him. "I can help you," he said. "I name you Seeing Buffalo."

Almost instantly, the buffalo bellowed with joy. He could see again! But now Jumping Mouse could not see. He had become a donor, giving his sight to the buffalo. But he had not realized that helping the buffalo would mean the sacrifice of his own sight.

"You have given me a gift of great value," said Seeing Buffalo. "Hold on to my shaggy fur and I will guide you."

When they got to the far-off land, Jumping Mouse said good-bye to his friend. Seeing Buffalo wished him well.

Jumping Mouse now went very slowly, sniffing and feeling his way. "I must not give up hope. I must not give up hope," he said. But tears ran down his cheeks. Exhausted, he stopped.

At that moment, Jumping Mouse heard a familiar voice.

"Do not be afraid," Frog said. "Your unselfish spirit has brought you to the far-off land."

Then he heard Frog commanding him again. "Jump! Jump up as high as you can." Jumping Mouse did. He let the wind carry him higher and higher into the sky. As he rose, he regained his sight. He looked down and saw the beautiful earth below him.

"Now," Frog said, "you have a new name. Now you are Eagle."

WHAT DO YOU THINK?

Do you think Jumping Mouse will enjoy being an eagle? Why or why not?

When Tonya's Friends Come to Spend the Night

by Eloise Greenfield

When Tonya's friends come
to spend the night
Her mama's more than just polite
She says she's glad they came to call
Tells them that she loves them all
Listens to what they can do
Tells them what she's good at, too
Plays her horn and lets them sing
(Do they make that music swing!)
Feeds them sweet banana bread
Hugs them when it's time for bed
Tonya sure would have a gripe
If she were the jealous type
But she isn't just a guest
She knows her mama loves her best

The Bench

by Martha Morss

High on a hill
in my favorite park
is a long green bench
where we sit and talk
and admire the view . . .

a gift from someone we never knew.

On the bench: DONATED BY THE MILLER FAMILY

4 YOU 2 DO

Word Play

Think up clue words to help a partner guess each vocabulary word below. For example, *knowing* could be a clue word for *aware*. Give your partner up to four clues.

- aware
- compassion
- donor
- missions
- sacrifice
- unselfish
- value

Making Connections

How might Jumping Mouse reach out to people? Would he train a therapy dog, join the National Guard, or donate an organ? Why do you think as you do?

On Paper

Write about one way you could give your talents, time, or effort to help others.

Contents

We the People...

110

Words 2 the Wise

Our Constitution begins with the phrase "We the people." As you read, think about why **protecting freedom** is important.

Let's Explore

FRE

The Liberty Bell and the Statue of Liberty are two symbols of freedom.

What is freedom? Freedom means that you are not controlled by anyone else. You can have your own ideas. You can speak up for what you believe. You will be treated fairly. There are many ways to protect our freedom. We protect our freedom by having rights, laws, and celebrations.

EDOM

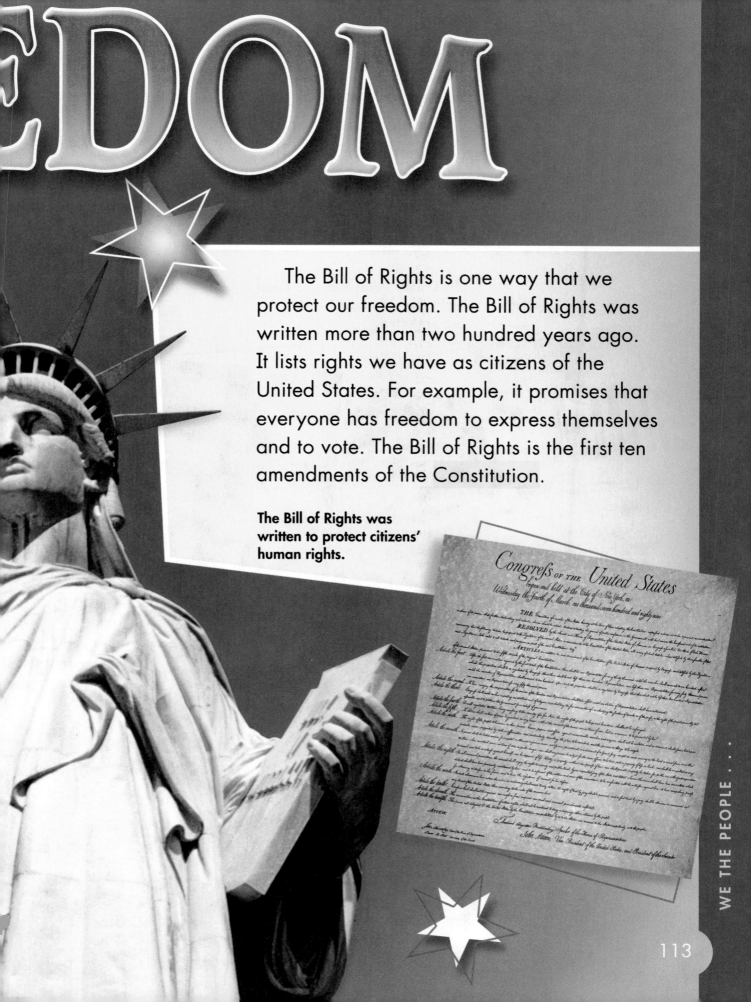

The Bill of Rights is one way that we protect our freedom. The Bill of Rights was written more than two hundred years ago. It lists rights we have as citizens of the United States. For example, it promises that everyone has freedom to express themselves and to vote. The Bill of Rights is the first ten amendments of the Constitution.

The Bill of Rights was written to protect citizens' human rights.

The Constitution explains the laws that protect our freedom. It tells how our government must be set up. These laws help protect our rights. They help make this country safe. The Bill of Rights and the Constitution protect our rights to protest and to make changes when the laws are unfair.

The United States Supreme Court makes sure that our freedoms are protected.

This statue of Martin Luther King, Jr., in Birmingham, Alabama, is a reminder of the value of freedom.

Finally, we promote our freedom by celebrating. We celebrate holidays like Martin Luther King, Jr. Day, the Fourth of July, and Memorial Day. We have parades and festivals to celebrate. We also build statues and monuments. These celebrations remind us that we must work hard to keep our freedom.

OUTSIDE *Independence*

by Owen Thomas

In 1787 Philadelphia, Pennsylvania, was the nation's largest city. About 40,000 people lived there. On the busy cobblestone streets, you could see Native Americans, African Americans, Quaker merchants, and German farmers.

In 1787 the Federal Convention took place in Independence Hall in Philadelphia. Fifty-five men were delegates, or representatives, at the convention. They met and wrote the United States Constitution during one of the hottest summers in history.

Fifty-five men gathered to write the Constitution.

Hall

The Constitution would be a set of rules to guide the new United States government. The Constitution would protect the people's rights.

Outside Independence Hall, crowds waited. People did not want the delegates to give some people more rights than others. The citizens wanted the delegates to guarantee the same rights to every free person.

George Washington, Benjamin Franklin, and James Madison were three delegates at the convention.

George Washington

Benjamin Franklin

James Madison

The people waited anxiously for the delegates to finish.

The delegates spoke for the people. The government would be "of the people, by the people, and for the people." Were these men capable of this giant task?

The crowd in front of Independence Hall was excited. The delegates could not see the crowd. But they could hear them outside. Their shoes rattled loudly against the cobblestone.* How could the delegates work with that noise? The delegates had the cobblestones covered with dirt. Then it was quieter.

*cobblestone round stones that were used to pave streets

118

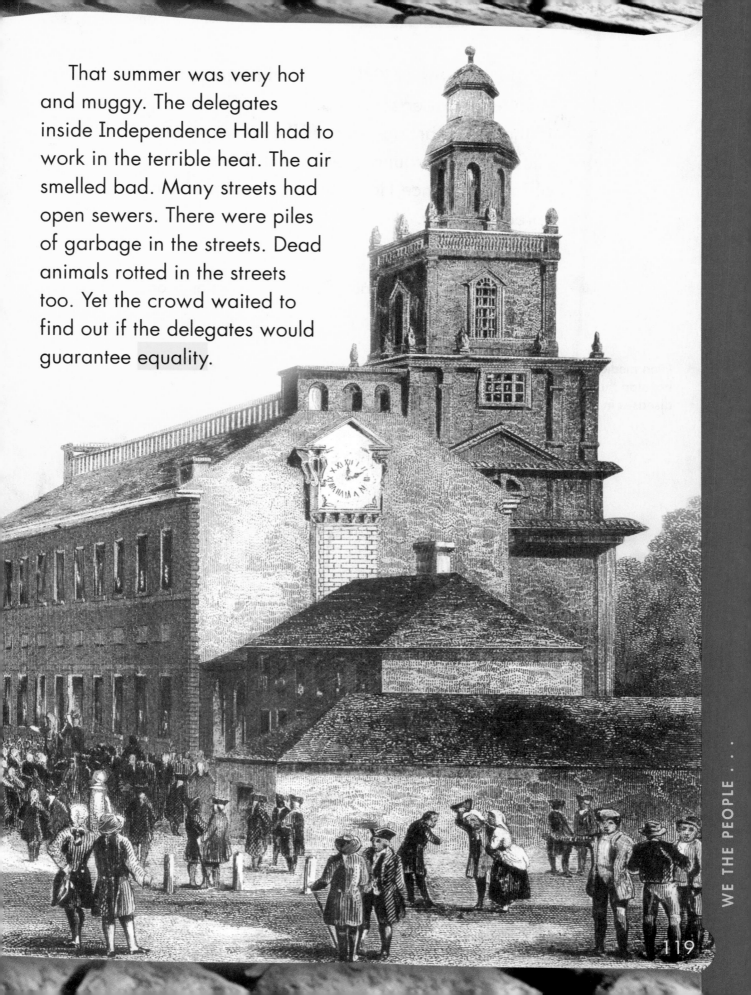

That summer was very hot and muggy. The delegates inside Independence Hall had to work in the terrible heat. The air smelled bad. Many streets had open sewers. There were piles of garbage in the streets. Dead animals rotted in the streets too. Yet the crowd waited to find out if the delegates would guarantee equality.

The citizens of Philadelphia had to worry about sickness. A disease called typhoid (TYE-foyd)* spread in the city. Garbage in open sewers attracted flies. Flies buzzed around everyone inside and outside of Independence Hall. Flies caused the disease to spread quickly.

*typhoid disease that is caused by dirty water and food

Even medical treatments could not stop the spread of certain diseases in the 1780s.

In the 1780s, there was no way to know if drinking water was clean.

A cool drink of water is a relief on a hot summer day. When the delegates wanted some water, they could not be sure that it was safe to drink. At that time, Philadelphia had no way to provide clean water. Citizens often drank dirty water.

Imagine how good a shower or bath feels when you're hot. In 1787 homes did not have running water. This made it difficult for people to bathe and wash their clothes.

Today children get rid of germs by washing often. People in the late 1700s did not wash often. They covered up the smell of sweat with powder and perfume. Sweet scents did not prevent disease. In fact, the flies that spread typhoid may have bitten people because they wore perfume.

There were no showers, and bathtubs weren't common in the 1700s. Most people used a washbowl and pitcher.

In spite of the heat and disease, the delegates completed the United States Constitution. They agreed that citizens were equal. They agreed that citizens could vote for their leaders. This made the Constitution different from the constitutions of other governments. Equality and voting rights were not common at that time.

The delegates in Philadelphia were successful. The Constitution was completed on September 17, 1787.

What Do You Think?

The United States Constitution protects and promotes our freedom. It is one of our most important documents.

What happened after the delegates started to work at Independence Hall?

When the Redcoat

by Orinda Robertson
illustrated by Doris Ettlinger

"Pa, let me help you fight the British," Adam pleaded.

His father shook his head. "No, son. Your job is at home because brave men are needed here too."

As Adam watched his father leave their homestead*, he shook his head angrily. How could he fight for freedom by doing chores? He stomped to the barn.

He collected wood until his mother called him.

"Adam," she nervously said. "British soldiers have arrived."

*homestead a farm
and its buildings

Came

"Redcoats!" Adam snarled. "Why are they here?"

"Be careful," his mother warned. "Be polite to them."

Adam watched as British soldiers forced their way in. They shoved furniture around and ordered Adam to bring food.

He had to obey because of British laws. Colonists were forced to let British soldiers live in their houses, but colonists could not stand it. *No wonder colonists called these laws the Intolerable Acts,* Adam thought. This treatment was intolerable!

After a long, tense week, the soldiers left. The family was relieved because the house did not feel livable when the soldiers took it over.

That night, a group of men knocked on the door. When he opened the door, Adam recognized many of his neighbors.

"Adam," Daniel said. "Your father gave us permission to meet here."

"Us?" Adam asked.

"Yes," Daniel said, glancing over his shoulder, "The Minute Men." His voice was barely audible.*

*audible loud enough to be heard

126

Adam's eyes widened as he remembered what
he had heard about the Minute Men. They were
ordinary citizens, but they were ready in a minute
to fight the British. They shared the same dream of
building a new nation.

"How can I help?" Adam asked eagerly.

"Hide us. The Redcoats are everywhere!"

"Count on me," Adam said.

Soon thirty men were inside, talking of strategies
and battles.

The next night, Adam heard a knock. Tap-tap.
TAP! That knock was a code. It told Adam and his
family that the visitor was one of the Minute Men.
He needed a safe place to stay. The family hid him
until he left the next morning. Adam had forgotten
his disappointment about having to stay home. He
wasn't fighting in battles like his father was. But he
was proud to fight for freedom in his own way!

The Minute Men held meetings at Adam's house all the time. Adam guarded the door each time. One night, Adam noticed Redcoats marching up to the door. He gave a quiet whistle. The men inside scattered quickly, leaving no sign that they had been there. Adam quickly began to tend the fire, and his mother stirred the kettle.

The British burst in the front door with their guns out, shouting orders. Adam stepped in front of his mother and sister.

"Where are the traitors?" the British captain asked.

"There are no traitors in this house, sir," Adam said.

"We have been watching this house. Men are having meetings here," the soldier said. "If you hide traitors, you will be punished!"

"What meetings?" Adam said.

"Don't act foolish, boy," the soldier said sharply. "These men are dangerous!"

"You mean my neighbors? They are helping us while my father is away," Adam replied confidently.

The Redcoats searched the house. They found no one. The soldiers marched away, and Adam and his mother breathed easily again.

Now Adam understood what his father meant. Hiding the Minute Men was not fighting, but it was dangerous. He was doing his part for freedom. As he went out to chop logs, Adam thought of his father and hoped that he was safe. Now they both could share stories of courage in their fight for independence.

What Do You Think?

When do Adam's feelings about staying home begin to change?

PROTECT *Our* PAST

The Constitution is over 200 years old! The Constitution, the Declaration of Independence, and the Bill of Rights are all written on parchment. Parchment is made from sheepskin.

Did you know that some documents have to stay locked inside top-secret vaults at night? It's true!

The Constitution, the Bill of Rights, and the Declaration of Independence are some of those documents. The founding fathers of the United States wrote these papers over 200 years ago! They each promise freedom and equality for all Americans.

You can find them on display at the National Archives in Washington, D.C.

The Bill of Rights, the Declaration of Independence, and the Constitution are in display cases at the National Archives for everyone to see.

TING

But how are they kept safe?

Visitors at the National Archives have to go through metal detectors and have their bags X-rayed. Guards watch everything with cameras.

The documents are on display in cases made of titanium* (ty-TAY-nee-uhm) and very strong glass. Scientists filled the cases with a gas called argon. No outside air can get inside the cases. Air might damage the documents.

At night, robotic arms move the documents to three secret vaults made of "super concrete." There, they are safe from thieves and even natural disasters!

*titanium a strong, lightweight metal
that has a silver-gray color

Here you can see a bag being X-rayed. Guards can see what's inside without even opening it.

4 FOR YOU 2 Do

Word Play

Unscramble these words to find some of this week's concept vocabulary.

TLQUYEAI

EMOREFD

TSBETLA

Making Connections

The delegates who wrote the Constitution and Adam had big responsibilities. How did each of them help protect freedom?

On Paper

What freedoms do you have? Choose one and tell about it.

Answers for Word Play: equality, freedom, battles

Glossary

as·sist·ance (ə sis′ təns), *NOUN.* help; aid: *After she was hurt in the soccer game, she needed assistance to get off the field.*

a·ware (ə wâr′), *ADJECTIVE.* having information: *She was not aware of the danger she faced.*

bat·tle (bat′ l), *NOUN.*
  1 a fight between armies or air forces: *The battle for the island lasted six months.*
  2 any fight or contest: *The candidates fought a battle of words during the campaign.* PL. **bat·tles.**

a in hat	ō in open	sh in she
ā in age	ȯ in all	th in thin
â in care	ô in order	ŦH in then
ä in far	oi in oil	zh in measure
e in let	ou in out	ə =a in about
ē in equal	u in cup	ə =e in taken
ėr in term	u̇ in put	ə =i in pencil
i in it	ü in rule	ə =o in lemon
ī in ice	ch in child	ə =u in circus
o in hot	ng in long	

ben·e·fi·cial (ben′ ə fish′ əl), ADJECTIVE. helpful: *Daily exercise is beneficial to your health.*

char·i·ty (char′ ə tē), NOUN.
  1 giving to people in need: *The charity of citizens enabled the hospital to purchase new beds.*
  2 a fund or organization for helping people in need: *She gives money to a charity that helps homeless people.*

com·pas·sion (kəm pash′ ən), NOUN. a feeling of being sorry for someone else's hardship and wanting to help; sympathy: *Her compassion for people with hearing problems led her to study sign language.*

con·sid·er·ate (kən sid′ ər it), ADJECTIVE. thoughtful of other people and their feelings: *It was considerate of you to call and let me know that you would be late.*

con·sti·tu·tion (kon′ stə tü′ shən), NOUN.
  1 a system of rules by which a nation, state, or group is governed: *Each state has its own constitution.*
  2 the Constitution, the written set of basic rules by which the United States is governed: *Delegates met in Pennsylvania to write the U.S. Constitution.*

cou·ra·geous (kə rā′ jəs), ADJECTIVE. fearless; not afraid of danger: *She was very courageous to stand up to the bully.*

dis·tress (dis tres′), NOUN. great pain or suffering; trouble: *The loss of her kitten caused her great distress.*

do·nate (dō′ nāt), VERB. to give money or help: *I will donate ten dollars to charity.*

do·nor (dō′ nər), NOUN. someone who donates: *A blood donor is a person who gives blood.*

a in hat	ō in open	sh in she
ā in age	ȯ in all	th in thin
â in care	ô in order	ᵺ in then
ä in far	oi in oil	zh in measure
e in let	ou in out	ə =a in about
ē in equal	u in cup	ə =e in taken
ėr in term	ù in put	ə =i in pencil
i in it	ü in rule	ə =o in lemon
ī in ice	ch in child	ə =u in circus
o in hot	ng in long	

e·mer·gen·cy (i mėr′ jən sē), NOUN. a situation that calls for something to be done right away: *Firefighters are often called to the scene of an emergency.* PL. **e·mer·gen·cies.**

e·qual·i·ty (i kwäl′ ə tē), NOUN. being equal; having the same rights: *Martin Luther King Jr. worked for equality for all people.*

ex·cur·sion (ek skėr′ zhən), NOUN. a short trip: *We took an excursion into the mountains last weekend.*

for·tu·nate (fôr′ chə nit), ADJECTIVE. having luck; lucky: *You are fortunate to have such a large playground at your school.*

free·dom (frē′ dəm), NOUN. being able to make your own choices; not controlled by anyone else: *The American colonists gained freedom from England.*

gov·ern·ment (guv′ ərn mənt), *NOUN.* a group of people that rules or manages a country, state, district, or city at any time: *The President, the Congress, and the Supreme Court make up the U.S. government.*

guar·an·tee (gar′ ən tē′), *VERB.* to promise to do something: *The store will guarantee that my purchase is delivered by Friday.*

im·prove (im prüv′), *VERB.* to make or become better: *Reading can help you improve your spelling.* **im·proved, im·prov·ing.**

a in hat	ō in open	sh in she
ā in age	ȯ in all	th in thin
â in care	ô in order	ŦH in then
ä in far	oi in oil	zh in measure
e in let	ou in out	ə =a in about
ē in equal	u in cup	ə =e in taken
ėr in term	u̇ in put	ə =i in pencil
i in it	ü in rule	ə =o in lemon
ī in ice	ch in child	ə =u in circus
o in hot	ng in long	

in·ter·vene (in tər′ vēn), *VERB.* to come between: *The teacher had to intervene in the argument between Helen and Mark.* **in·ter·vened, in·ter·ven·ing.**

in·tol·er·a·ble (in tol′ ər ə bəl), *ADJECTIVE.* too hard or painful to stand: *The pain from my sore tooth was intolerable!*

in·trin·sic (in trin′ zik), *ADJECTIVE.* belonging to a thing naturally: *An intrinsic quality of my sister is her kindness.*

mis·sion (mish′ ən), *NOUN.* an errand or task that people are sent to do: *He was sent on a mission to find the lost treasure.* *PL.* **mis·sions.**

or·gan·i·za·tion (ôr′ gə nə zā′ shən), *NOUN.* a group of people that comes together for a purpose: *The organization raises money to help fight cancer.*

pan·ic (pan′ ik), *NOUN.* sudden uncontrollable feeling of fear that could cause a person or group to lose control: *When the elevator suddenly stopped between floors, riders were filled with panic.*

pose (pōz), *VERB.* to pretend to be something or someone else: *He posed as a king although he was a servant.* **posed, pos·ing.**

re·lief (ri lēf′), *NOUN.* help given to people in the form of food, clothing, or money: *Relief in the form of food and blankets was quickly sent to the tornado victims.*

re·u·nite (rē yü nīt′), *VERB.* to bring together again; come together again: *The band members planned to reunite for a concert after being apart for ten years.* **re·u·nit·ed, re·u·nit·ing.**

a in hat	ō in open	sh in she
ā in age	ȯ in all	th in thin
â in care	ô in order	ŦH in then
ä in far	oi in oil	zh in measure
e in let	ou in out	ə =a in about
ē in equal	u in cup	ə =e in taken
ėr in term	u̇ in put	ə =i in pencil
i in it	ü in rule	ə =o in lemon
ī in ice	ch in child	ə =u in circus
o in hot	ng in long	

risk•y (ris′ kē), _ADJECTIVE._ full of danger or risk: _Skydiving is a risky sport._ **risk•i•er, risk•i•est.**

sac•ri•fice (sak′ rə fīs),

   1 _NOUN._ the act of giving up one thing for another: _Staying after school to practice for the talent show instead of meeting up with friends was a big sacrifice._
   2 _VERB._ to give up something: _My mother will sacrifice her free time to help at the blood drive this afternoon._ **sac•ri•fic•es, sac•ri•fic•ed, sac•ri•fic•ing.**

strand (strand), _VERB._ to leave in a helpless position: _She was stranded hundreds of miles from home with a broken-down car and no money._ **strand•ed, strand•ing.**

sup·port (sə pôrt′),

1 *NOUN.* help; aid: *The team needs the fans' support to win.*

2 *VERB.* to provide help or aid: *She donated her hair to support Locks of Love.* **sup·port·ed, sup·port·ing.**

un·self·ish (un sel′ fish), *ADJECTIVE.* caring about the needs of other people; generous: *She is an unselfish person.*

val·ue (val′ yü), *NOUN.*

1 the real worth of something in money: *We bought the house for less than its value.*

2 the usefulness or importance of something: *The value of homework becomes clear when it is time to take the test.*

a in hat	ō in open	sh in she
ā in age	ȯ in all	th in thin
â in care	ô in order	ŦH in then
ä in far	oi in oil	zh in measure
e in let	ou in out	ə =a in about
ē in equal	u in cup	ə =e in taken
ėr in term	u̇ in put	ə =i in pencil
i in it	ü in rule	ə =o in lemon
ī in ice	ch in child	ə =u in circus
o in hot	ng in long	

Acknowledgments

Text

Every effort has been made to locate the copyright owner of material reproduced in this component. Omissions brought to our attention will be corrected in subsequent editions. Grateful acknowledgment is made to the following for copyrighted material.

104 Dial Books for Young Readers, A division of Penguin Group (USA), Inc. "When Tonya's Friends Come to Spend the Night" by Eloise Greenfield from *Night on Neighborhood Street*. Text Copyright © 1991 by Eloise Greenfield. Used by permission of Dial Books for Young Readers, a Division of Penguin Young Readers Group, a Member of Penguin Group (USA) Inc., 345 Hudson Street, New York, NY 10014. All rights reserved.

104–105 Herman Agency "When Tonya's Friends Come to Spend the Night" by Eloise Greenfield from *Night on Neighborhood Street*. Text Copyright © 1991 by Eloise Greenfield. Pictures copyright © 1991 by Jan Spivey Gilchrist (Dial Books for Young Readers). All rights reserved. Used by permission.

Illustrations

6, 28, 29 Bill Vann; 20–26 Philip Williams; 37 Susan J. Carlson; 70–77 Meredith Johnson; 96–102 Mike Reed; 104, 106 Kathleen Kemly; 110, 124–131 Doris Ettlinger.

Photographs

Every effort has been made to secure permission and provide appropriate credit for photographic material. The publisher deeply regrets any omission and pledges to correct errors called to its attention in subsequent editions. Unless otherwise acknowledged, all photographs are the property of Pearson Education, Inc. Photo locators denoted as follows: Top (T), Center (C), Bottom (B), Left (L), Right (R), Background (Bkgd)

Cover: (CR) ©Gwendolyn Mambo/Alamy, (BR) ©Make-A-Wish Foundation of America, Frank Siteman/Getty Images, (TL) Getty Images, (CR) Monkey Business/Fotolia; **1** (CL) Getty Images; **2** (BR) Jim Sugar/Corbis, (CR) Left Lane Productions/Corbis; **3** (BR) ©Royalty-Free/Corbis, (TL) Derek Berwin/Getty Images; **5** (Bkgd) Getty Images, (CR) Monkey Business/Fotolia; **6** (CR) ©Powerhouse Digital Photography Ltd/Alamy, (Bkgd) Getty Images; **7** (L) Getty Images; **8** (Bkgd) Getty Images, (BC) Left Lane Productions/Corbis; **9** (TC) Baerbel Schmidt/Getty Images; **10** (TR) Jeff Greenberg/AGE Fotostock, (CL) Jim West/Alamy; **11** Dynamic Graphics Group/i2i/Alamy Images; **12** (TL, Bkgd) Getty Images; **13** (CR, C, BR, B) ©Courtesy of Locks of Love, (T) AP/Wide World Photos; **14** (T) David Lane/Palm Beach Post/Zuma Press, Inc., (Bkgd) Getty Images; **15** (CL) ZUMA Press, Inc./Alamy, (BR) Scott Barbour/Getty Images; **16** (B) Bob Daemmrich/Corbis, (BR) ©Powerhouse Digital Photography Ltd/Alamy, (Bkgd) Getty Images; **17** (T) AP/Wide World Photos, (CR) Getty Images; **18** (B) ©Make-A-Wish Foundation of America, (TL, Bkgd) Getty Images; **19** (TR) ©Make-A-Wish Foundation of America, (TL) Chuck Green/Zuma Press, Inc., (TC) Copyright 2006 NBAE/Getty Images, (BC) Getty Images; **28** (BL) Getty Images; **29** (TR, BR) Getty Images; **30** (R, Bkgd) Getty Images; **31** epa/Corbis; **32** (CR) PhotoAlto/Getty Images, (TR) Roger Archibald/IPN, (CR) Stephanie Sinclair/Corbis, (BR) Steven Puetzer/Getty Images; **33** (L) JLP/Sylvia Torres/Corbis; **34** (Bkgd) Jim Sugar/Corbis, (BC) Roger Archibald/IPN; **35** (BL) Michael Freeman/Corbis; **36** (B) Corbis, (T) Getty Images, (TL) ©Picture Contac BV/Alamy Images; **38** (B) Philippe Desmazes/Getty Images; **39** (TL) Kieran Doherty/Reuters/Corbis, (CR) Stephanie Sinclair/Corbis; **40** (TR) ©Picture Contac BV/Alamy Images, (CL) Patrick Robert/Sygma/Corbis; **41** (BC) Ian Berry/©Magnum Photos; **42** (BC) Hoang Dinh Nam/Getty Images; **43** (L) Ian Berry/©Magnum Photos; **44** (TL, BR) Hemera Technologies; **45** (L) ©Clinton Collection/Clements Library, University of Michigan, (Bkgd) Getty Images, (BR) The Granger Collection, New York; **46** (T) Corbis; **47** (BR) Courtesy Archives of Michigan; **48** (L) Bettmann/Corbis; **49** ©Bettmann/Corbis; **50** (BL) Records of the Office of Strategic Services/National Archives; **51** (BR) Hemera Technologies, (BL) PhotoAlto/Getty Images; **52** (BL) Robin Lynne Gibson/Getty Images; **53** (TL) Peter Cade/Getty Images, (TR, CL, BR) Steven Puetzer/Getty Images; **54** (BL) Trisha Cluck/Getty Images; **55** (T) Getty Images; **56** (BR) JLP/Sylvia Torres/Corbis; **57** (L) ©Royalty-Free/Corbis, (Bkgd) Derek Berwin/Getty Images; **58** (BR) ©American Red Cross, (C) Getty Images, (CR) Brendan Fitterer/Tampa Bay Times/ZUMAPRESS.com; **60** (Bkgd) ©Joson/zefa/Corbis, (B) AP/Wide World Photos; **61** (T) ©Jane Sapinsky/SuperStock, (BL) ©Tom Payne/Alamy; **62** (BR) Image provided by ORBIMAGE. ©Orbital Imaging Corporation and processing by NASA Goddard Space Flight Center., (T) Michelle Pacitto/Shutterstock, (Bkgd) Reza; Webistan/Corbis; **63** (TL) Frank Siteman/Getty Images; **64** (Bkgd) Alejandro Ernesto/epa/Corbis, (T) Reuters/Corbis; **65** (BR) EPA/John Riley/Landov LLC; **66** (TC) Chris Graythen/Getty Images, (Bkgd) Michelle Pacitto/Shutterstock; **67** (BC) Reuters/Corbis; **68** (BC) Brendan Fitterer/Tampa Bay Times/ZUMAPRESS.com, (Bkgd) Viviane Moos/Corbis; **69** (CL) AP/Wide World Photos; **78** (CR) ©American Red Cross, (CL) Courtesy of FEMA, (BL) James Pinsky/U.S. Navy/Zuma/Corbis, (BR) Reuters/Corbis; **79** (CL) ©AmeriCares Foundation, (CR) ©NOVA, (BL) William Foley/Getty Images; **80** (TL) ©America's Second Harvest—The Nation's Food Bank Network, (L) ©Tim Boyle/Getty Images, (TR) DK Images, (CR) Erik S. Lesser/Getty Images, (TR) Habitat for Humanity International, (TR) Hemera Technologies, (BL) Najlah Feanney/Corbis; **81** (TL) ©Salvation Army National Headquarters, (TR) ©United Way of America, (TC) Hemera Technologies, (CL) Pegaz/Alamy Images; **82** (R) ©Royalty-Free/Corbis; **83** (C) ©Asia Images Group/Getty Images; **84** (CR) ©Myrleen Ferguson Cate/PhotoEdit, Inc., (CR) Samuel King Jr./Courtesy of The National Guard Bureau; **85** (CL) Mark Olsen/Courtesy of The National Guard Bureau; **87** (BR) ©Myrleen Ferguson Cate/PhotoEdit, Inc.; **88** (C) ©Myrleen Ferguson Cate/PhotoEdit, Inc.; **89** (T) ©Gwendolyn Mambo/Alamy; **90** (TR) StockphotoPro, Inc., (B) ©Walter Panda/Alamy; **91** (C, B) Courtesy of The National Guard Bureau; **92** (C) ©Matt Rainey/Corbis; **93** (T) Samuel King Jr./Courtesy of The National Guard Bureau; **94** (C) ©Kris Timken/Getty Images; **95** (T) ©Jack Hollingsworth/Getty Images; **108** (BR) Mark Olsen/Courtesy of The National Guard Bureau; **109** Jake Rajs/Getty Images; **110** (BR) ©Dennis MacDonald/Alamy, (CR) ©Royalty-Free/Corbis, (TR) Ian Dagnall/Alamy Images; **111** (L) Richard T. Nowitz/Corbis; **112** (CL) Ian Dagnall/Alamy Images; **113** (L) Getty Images, (BR) The Granger Collection, NY; **114** (CR) Bettmann/Corbis, (Bkgd) Firefly Productions/Corbis, (CL) Getty Images; **115** (TR) Jeff Greenberg/Alamy Images; **116** (B) ©Bettmann/Corbis, (Bkgd) ©Eduardo Garcia/Getty Images; **117** (TR) Bettmann/Corbis, (BR) Reunion des Musees Nationaux/Art Resource, NY, (CR) The Corcoran Gallery of Art/Corbis; **118** (Bkgd) ©Eduardo Garcia/Getty Images, The Granger Collection, NY; **120** (B) The Granger Collection, NY; **121** (BC) Hemera Technologies, (TR) North Wind Picture Archives; **122** (Bkgd) ©Eduardo Garcia/Getty Images, (B) Nancy Carter/North Wind Picture Archives; **123** (B) ©Royalty-Free/Corbis; **132** (BL) ©Dennis MacDonald/Alamy, (T) Dream Maker Software, (CL) Steve Bronstein/Getty Images; **133** (BR) Ace Stock Limited/Alamy Images; **134** (BR) Richard T. Nowitz/Corbis; **135** (C) Left Lane Productions/Corbis; **136** (BR) The Granger Collection, NY; **137** (C) Pegaz/Alamy Images; **138** (TR) Derek Berwin/Getty Images; **139** (C) ©Bettmann/Corbis; **140** (B) Bob Daemmrich/Corbis; **141** (CR) Reuters/Corbis; **142** (T) Roger Archibald/IPN; **143** (T) ©Courtesy of Locks of Love.